THE WISDOM OF MOTHER TERESA

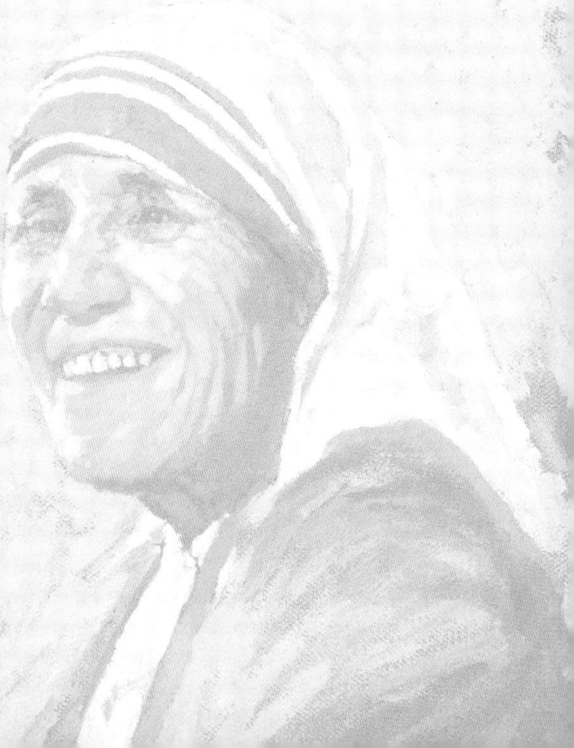

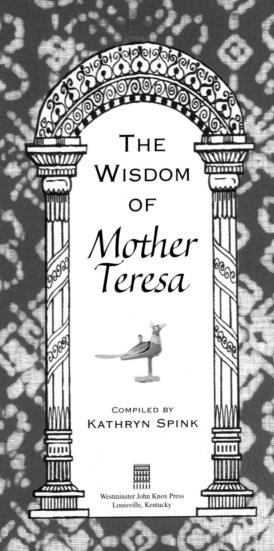

THE
WISDOM
OF
Mother Teresa

COMPILED BY
KATHRYN SPINK

Westminster John Knox Press
Louisville, Kentucky

Text © 1998.
Original edition published in English under the title
The Wisdom of Mother Teresa by Lion Publishing plc, Oxford,
England. Copyright © Lion Publishing plc 1998.

Design by Philippa Jenkins
Cover and first page illustration by David Axtell

Published by Westminster John Knox Press, 2000
Louisville, Kentucky

00 01 02 03 04 05 06 07 08 09 -- 10 9 8 7 6 5 4 3 2 1

A catalog card for this book may be obtained
from the Library of Congress

ISBN 0-664-22212-9

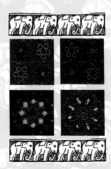

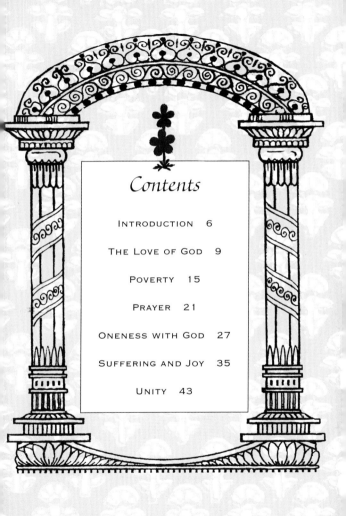

Contents

INTRODUCTION

Agnes Gonxha Bojaxhiu was born on 26 August 1910 in Skopje, Yugoslavia, the youngest child of devoutly Roman Catholic parents. Her father died when Agnes was only nine years old. Consequently it was largely under the influence of her mother's insistence on the value of the non-material riches of kindness, generosity and compassion for the poor and weak, and the importance of prayer and love in the home, that the foundations for Agnes's future apostolate were laid.

In 1928 she applied to join the Loreto Sisters and for eighteen years taught in Loreto schools in Calcutta until, in September 1946 while on a train travelling to a retreat in Darjeeling, she experienced what she herself referred to as 'a call within a call'. It was an experience about which Mother Teresa said little. The message was, nevertheless, unambiguous: 'I was to leave the convent and help the poor while living among them. It was an order. To fail it would have been to break the faith.'

In obedience to this call, in 1948 she stepped out into some of the world's most disease-ridden slums to live as one with the poorest of the poor and found a Congregation committed to their service. The Congregation of the Missionaries of Charity, formally erected on 7 October 1950, would take, in addition to the traditional vows of poverty, chastity and obedience, a fourth very specific vow of 'wholehearted free service to the poorest of the poor'. In those 'poorest of the poor' Mother Teresa identified the hungry, thirsty, lonely, imprisoned Christ of Matthew's Gospel, the Christ who had specifically said: 'Whatsoever you did to the least of these my brothers, you did it to me.' In every chapel of the Missionaries of Charity are inscribed the two words, 'I thirst'. The profound calling of the Order is to quench the thirst of Christ on the cross for love and souls.

In time Mother Teresa's recognition of who constituted the poor, in whom Christ in his distressing disguise still thirsted, grew. The work which began in the Calcutta slums with the creation of small schools where she scratched the alphabet in the dust, led to the opening of children's homes; homes for the dying; mobile and static leprosy clinics; homes for the victims of AIDS, and a multitude of other attempts to alleviate the world's suffering. Her mission spread wherever her particular geography of compassion identified a need.

Increased contact with the materially rich West brought Mother Teresa to the understanding that its spiritual poverty was more problematic than the physical poverty of the so-called 'Third World'. In materially richer societies she saw the breakdown of family life, and in response she called increasingly for people to make their homes 'another Nazareth'. She set about meeting the 'hunger and the thirst' of those who sometimes did not even recognize their own poverty, by making them more fully aware not only of the need, but also of the spiritual riches of the materially poor. She wanted the rich to save the poor and the poor to save the rich. She appealed to those who in a material sense had plenty, to give – not from their abundance, but until it hurt.

By the time Mother Teresa died on 5 September 1997, her Missionaries of Charity were in over 120 countries. She left a legacy of some 4,000 Sisters, and countless Missionary of Charity Brothers and Fathers, lay Missionaries of Charity, Co-Workers and other volunteers scattered throughout the world. Mother Teresa, who was remembered by her contemporaries at Loreto for her goodness and conscientiousness but for little more than benign ordinariness, had become a household name. Her life was not devoid of criticism; her views on such issues as birth control, abortion and the role of women were uncompromising. Yet people of all nationalities, creeds and denominations have been prepared to recognize her as a 'holy person', for she for her part insisted on respect for the way in which God was present and at work in every human soul.

Mother Teresa was not one who came to know God through clear images and careful thought. Hers was an understanding of the heart. The vision she holds out to us is of Christ crying out for love in the broken bodies of the poor and of Christ simultaneously offering himself as spiritual sustenance in order that that cry might not go without response. She was not an intellectual. She spoke in the simple language of an apparently unquestioningly obedient faith. Her response to poverty was invariably practical. Those who came to her seeking to understand were put to work because love was 'best proved in deeds', but also because experience taught her that it was often in action that real understanding and unity between people of different world views was born. The recognition she received she regarded as recognition of God's poor. The achievement was not hers but God's. When people acclaimed her as a saint she insisted that sanctity was not something far removed from the everyday. Holiness was what she asked of her Sisters – who were to be 'contemplatives in the world' in daily contact with the real living person of Jesus – but holiness was also a simple duty for everyone. 'Fidelity in small things' was a principle accessible to all, and even the smallest and least perfect things could be transformed by love. Her own secret was, she maintained, quite simple: it lay in the primacy she afforded to love and the open-hearted prayer which made that love possible.

KATHRYN SPINK

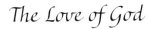

The Love of God

GOD SENT HIS SON
TO SATISFY THE
HUNGER OF THE
WORLD FOR LOVE.

God is love. He loves each one of us. We read
something beautiful in the Scriptures: 'I have
called you by your name, you are mine. Water will
not drown you, fire will not burn you, I will give up
nations for you, you are precious to me, I love you.
Even if a mother could forget her child, I will not
forget you. I have carved you on the palm of my
hand.' This is God speaking to you and to me, to
that leper man and that alcoholic woman, to the
person with a mental handicap and to the little
child: 'You are precious to me. I love you.'

'YOU DID IT TO ME'

It was because God loved the world so much that he gave his Son to die for the world and Jesus said, 'I have loved you as the Father has loved me. Love one another as I have loved you.' The giving was from the Father, the giving was from the Son, and now the giving is from us: 'Whatever you did to the least of these my brothers you did it to me.' Remember the words of St Matthew's Gospel: 'I was hungry and you gave me no food. I was thirsty and you gave me no drink, I was a stranger and you did not welcome me, naked and you did not clothe me, sick and in prison and you did not visit me.' God has identified himself with the hungry, the sick, the naked, the homeless, with those who hunger not just for bread but for love, for care, to be somebody to someone; with those who are naked not of clothing, but of that compassion that very few people give to those they do not know; with those who are homeless not just for a shelter made of stone but with that homelessness that comes from having no one to call your own.

Such is the delicate thoughtfulness of God that he made himself the Bread of Life that we might be able to eat and live, to satisfy our hunger for his love, and then he made himself the hungry one so that we – you and I – can satisfy his hunger for our love. We see Christ in the consecrated bread and we also see him in the broken bodies of the poor crying out for love. The biggest disease today is not leprosy or tuberculosis, but the feeling of being unwanted. People need to be loved. Without love, people die. But God is still love. He is still loving the world. Today God loves the world so much that he gives you and he gives me to love the world, to be his love and his compassion, his delicate thoughtfulness.

THE THIRST OF JESUS

Jesus, whose last words on the cross were 'I thirst', thirsts still for you. 'I thirst' is something much deeper than Jesus just saying, 'I love you.' The closer you come to Jesus, the better you will know his thirst. If you listen with your heart, you will hear and understand. 'Repent and believe', Jesus tells us. What are we to repent? Our indifference, our hardness of heart. What are we to believe? That Jesus thirsts even now, in your heart and in the poor. He is not bound by time. He knows your weakness. He wants only your love and the chance to love you.

5

LOVE IN ACTION

Every work of love, no matter how small, brings a person face to face with God. It is not the magnitude of our action that counts but the love we put into it. It is not how much we do that is pleasing to God but how much love we put into the doing. Love does not live on words, nor can it be explained by words, especially that love which serves him, which comes from him and which finds him and touches him. We must reach the heart, and to reach the heart love is proved in deeds.

Poverty

GIVE YOUR OWN
HANDS TO SERVE
CHRIST IN HIS POOR
AND YOUR HEARTS
TO LOVE HIM
IN THEM.

KNOWING THE POOR

Today once more when Jesus comes amongst his own, his own don't know him. And yet my poor ones in the world's slums are like the suffering Christ. In them God's son lives and dies, and through them God shows me his true face.

The least of God's brothers, the poorest of the poor, are: the hungry and lonely – not only for food, but also for the Word of God; the naked and unloved – not only for clothes but also for human dignity; the unwanted, the unborn child, the racially discriminated against, the homeless and abandoned – not only for a shelter made of bricks, but for a heart that understands, that covers and loves; the sick, the dying destitutes and the captives – not only in body but also in mind and spirit; all those who have lost faith in life, the alcoholics and drug addicts; all those who have lost God (for whom God was and not God is) and who have lost all hope in the power of the Spirit.

UNDERSTANDING POVERTY

I t is not enough to give from your abundance. In order really to understand you have to touch. To know the problem of poverty intellectually is not really to comprehend it. It is not by reading, taking a walk in the slums, admiring the spirit and regretting the misery that we get to understand it and to discover what it has of bad and good. We have to dive into it, live it, share it.

The very poor do not need words but actions. I cannot analyze systems, economic patterns and ideologies. There are in the world those who struggle for justice and for human rights and who try to change structures. We are not inattentive to this, but our daily contact is with people who do not even have a piece of bread to eat. Our mission is to look at the problem more individually and not collectively. We care for a person and not a multitude. We seek the person with whom Jesus Christ identified himself when he said, 'I was hungry, I was sick.' I recognize that each person has a conscience and must respond to its calling. Mine is this. So many times I have been told that I must not offer fishes to men but rods so that they can fish for themselves. Ah my God! So often they do not have the strength to hold the rods so that they can fish for themselves. Giving them fish I help them to recover the strength for the fishing of tomorrow.

The poor can be very wonderful people. As we tend to their broken bodies, often it is they who teach us. Sometimes we are brought face to face with our own poverty, with our own limitations and shortcomings, with self-knowledge. Self-knowledge puts us on our knees.

That is why we pray: 'Make us worthy, Lord, to serve our fellow men throughout the world who live and die in poverty and hunger.'

Prayer

PRAYER IS
BECOMING TWENTY-
FOUR HOURS A DAY
AT ONE WITH THE
WILL OF GOD.

Without prayer I could not work for even half an hour. I get my strength from God through prayer. You can pray while you work. Work does not stop prayer and prayer does not stop work. It requires only that small raising of the mind and heart to him: 'I love you God. I trust you. I believe in you. I need you now.' Small things like that are wonderful prayers. The poor are also our prayer. They carry God in them. Prayer means praying everything.

PRAYER OF THE HEART

Love to pray. Feel often during the day the need for prayer and take trouble to pray. Prayer enlarges the heart until it is capable of containing God's gift of himself. Ask and seek, turn to him at all times and your heart will grow big enough to receive him and keep him as your own. Try to be more in tune with God and more open to him, so that you will be able to see his face. Jesus said, 'Blessed are the pure in heart, for they shall see God.' We need to have an open heart to be able to see God in others.

When the time comes and we cannot pray, it is very simple – let Jesus pray in us to the Father in the silence of our hearts. If we cannot speak, he will speak. If we cannot pray, he will pray. So let us give him our inability and our nothingness. Prayer does not consist of many words but of the fervour of a heart turned towards God.

SILENCE

God is the friend of silence. If we really want to
pray we must first learn to listen, for in the
silence of the heart God speaks. God cannot be
found in noise and restlessness. See how nature,
the trees, the flowers, the grass, grow in perfect
silence. See the stars, the moon and the sun, how
they move in silence. The more we receive in silent
prayer, the more we can give in our active life.
In silence we will find new energy and true unity.
The energy of God will be ours to do all things
well. The unity of our thoughts with his thoughts,
the unity of our actions with his actions, of our life
with his life.

Oneness with God

'I WILL BE A SAINT'
MEANS I WILL DESPOIL
MYSELF OF ALL
THAT IS NOT GOD.

LIKE A CLEAR GLASS

Our souls should be like a clear glass through which God can be seen. Often this glass becomes spotted with dust and dirt. God can and will help us to remove the dirt and dust if we allow him to do it, with a sincere will to let him have his way. God longs to share his holiness with us: 'Be holy for I am holy.' We must long to receive it and this longing in itself is prayer. We have but to desire oneness with Christ.

15

SANCTITY

Sanctity is not the luxury of the few. It is a simple duty for you and for me. Sanctity is simply the acceptance of the will of God with a big smile. It is just accepting him as he comes into our life, accepting his taking from us whatever he wants, making use of us as he wants, putting us where he wants without our being consulted. We like to be consulted but he must be able to break us into pieces and let every little piece be his, empty without him.

Our progress in holiness depends on God and on ourselves: on God's grace and on our will to be holy. We must have a real living determination to reach holiness. 'I will be a saint' means I will despoil myself of all that is not God; I will strip my heart of all created things; I will live in poverty and detachment; I will renounce my will, my inclinations, my whims and fancies, and make myself a willing slave to the will of God.

TOTAL SURRENDER AND TRUST

One thing Jesus asks of me is that I lean upon him and surrender myself to him unreservedly. Even when I feel like a ship without a compass, I must give myself completely to him. I must not attempt to control God's actions. I must not desire a clear perception of my advance along the road. We are neither big nor small but what we are in the eyes of God, and as long as we surrender ourselves totally then God can use us. The emptier we are, the more room we give God to fill us. Even God cannot put anything into what is already full. By ourselves we may be able to do nothing but all the gifts of nature and grace can come from God. 'Father, into your hands I commend my spirit' – Jesus trusted his Father with an unshakeable trust and this is what we are called to do. His trust was the fruit of his intimate knowledge and love of the Father. He was fully confident that his Father would work out his plan of salvation in spite of the ineffectual means used and the apparent failure.

FIDELITY

When it is hard, remember we are not called to be successful but to be faithful. Fidelity is important in the least things, not for their own sake – for this is the work of small minds – but for the sake of the great thing which is the will of God. St Augustine said, 'Little things are indeed little, but to be faithful in little things is a great thing. Is not Our Lord equally the same in a small host as in a great one?'

19

SOMETHING BEAUTIFUL FOR GOD

The greatest fulfilment is in doing God's will.
We do not have to do great things, only small
things with great love. We do not have to be
extraordinary in any way. I can do what you can't
do and you can do what I can't do. Together we
can do something beautiful for God. We can be
the little pencils in the hand of God.

Suffering
and Joy

TODAY THE WORLD
IS AN OPEN CALVARY
BUT THE COMING OF
JESUS BRINGS JOY
TO EVERY HUMAN
HEART.

We cannot begin to understand the suffering of others unless we suffer ourselves. Pain and suffering have to come into our lives, but suffering begets life in the soul. It is a sign of love because this is how God the Father proved that he loved the world: by giving his Son to die for us and expiate our sin. The Spirit pours love, peace and joy into our hearts proportionately to our emptying ourselves of self-indulgence, vanity, anger and ambition, and to our willingness to shoulder the cross of Christ.

JESUS KNOWS YOUR PAIN

Jesus came amongst his own and his own received him not. He knew suffering and loneliness. He knows your pain. Bruised, divided, full of pain and wounds as you are, accept Jesus as he comes into your life and recognize him when once more he comes in his distressing disguise. Be not afraid in your suffering. God loves you. As miserable, weak and sinful as we are, he loves us with an infinitely faithful and forgiving love.

Without our suffering, our work would just be social work, very good and very helpful, but it would not be the work of Jesus Christ, not part of the Redemption. Jesus wanted to help us by sharing our life, our loneliness, our agony and death. All that he has taken upon himself and has carried into the darkest night. Only by being one with us has he redeemed us. We are allowed to do the same. All the desolation of the poor people, not only their material poverty, but their spiritual destitution must be redeemed by our being one with them. Suffering in itself is nothing, but suffering shared with Christ's passion can be a wonderful gift. Man's most beautiful gift is that he can share in the redemptive passion of Christ.

THE JOY OF THE RISEN CHRIST

Suffering, if it is accepted together, borne together, is joy. Remember that the passion of Christ ends always in the joy of the resurrection of Christ, so when you feel in your heart the suffering of Christ, remember the resurrection has to come. The joy of Easter has to dawn. Never let anything so fill you with sorrow as to make you forget the joy of the risen Christ.

In return for the great grace of baptism, the priest tells the newly baptized, 'May you serve the Church joyfully.' Joy is not simply a matter of temperament. Joy is often the mantle that hides a life of self-sacrifice. It is very infectious. The joy of Christ is our strength even if sometimes it is very hard to smile at one another. Joy is prayer, joy is strength, joy is love, joy is a net of love by which you can catch souls. God loves a cheerful giver. Whoever gives with joy gives most. The best way to show our gratitude to God and to people is to accept with joy.

HAPPY WITH GOD NOW

We all long for heaven where God is, but we have it in our power to be in heaven with him right now, to be happy with him at this very moment. But being happy with him now means loving as he loves, helping as he helps, giving as he gives, serving as he serves, rescuing as he rescues, being with him for all the twenty-four hours, touching him in his distressing disguise.

THE JOYFUL INSECURITY OF
DIVINE PROVIDENCE

Do not worry about tomorrow. Divine providence is wonderful. Christ has said that we are more important to his Father than the flowers of the field and the birds of the air and it is really true. St Augustine says: 'How can you doubt that God will give you good things since he vouchsafed to assume evil for you?' This must give us confidence in the providence of God who preserves even the birds and the flowers. Surely if God feeds the young ravens which cry to him, if he nourishes the birds which neither sow nor reap nor gather in barns, if he vests the flowers of the field so beautifully, how much more will he care for human beings whom he has made in his own image and likeness and adopted as his children, if we only act as such, keep his commandments and have confidence in him. Therefore be joyful in your insecurity. Just accept whatever he gives and give whatever he takes with a big smile.

Unity

LET US PREACH
THE PEACE OF CHRIST
AS HE DID.

We must all work in a small way for peace. We must learn from Jesus to be kind and humble of heart for only humility can bring us to unity and unity to peace. Cardinal Newman wrote: 'Help me to spread your fragrance everywhere I go. Let me preach you without preaching, not by words but by my example; by the catching force, the sympathetic influence of what I do, the evident fullness of the love my heart bears to you.' Peace begins with an ordinary example. It begins with a smile.

FORGIVENESS

The world has never needed more love and forgiveness than it does today. Think of the oppressed countries. There is so much bitterness and hatred as a consequence of what has been suffered. The greatest need is for forgiveness. If they could feel that someone cares about them, that they are loved, perhaps they would find it in their hearts to forgive in their turn. Whatever our belief, we must learn to forgive if we want truly to love. If we remember that we ourselves are sinners and have need of forgiveness, it is easy to forgive others. Unless I have realized this, it is very difficult for me to say, 'I forgive you.' We must make our homes, especially, centres of compassion and forgive endlessly.

'COME TO ME'

In the Gospel we often see one word: 'come to me all', 'he that cometh to me I will not cast out', 'suffer little children to come to me'. We must be always ready to unite, to receive, to forgive, to love and to make sure we understand what God means when he says, 'I say to you, as long as you did it to one of the least of my brothers, you did it to me.' Be kind and merciful. Let no one ever come to you without leaving better and happier. Be the living expression of God's kindness – kindness in your face, kindness in your eyes, kindness in your smile, kindness in your warm greeting. To children, to the poor, to all who suffer and are lonely, give always a happy smile. Give them not only your care but also your heart.

GOD DOES NOT FORCE HIMSELF

Faith is a gift of God but God does not force himself. He has his own ways and means to work in the hearts of men and we do not know how close they are to him, but by their actions we will always know whether they are at his disposal or not. Whether you are a Hindu, a Moslem or a Christian, how you live your life is the proof that you are fully his or not. We must not condemn or judge or pass words that will hurt people. We do not know what way God is appearing to that soul. I know only that at the hour of our death we shall be judged on what we have done for and to the unwanted, the unloved, the untouchables, the AIDS sufferers, all those who have lost all hope and faith in life and who look to us for comfort. And then there will be only two ways: 'come' or 'go'.

TEXT ACKNOWLEDGMENTS

Extracts have been drawn from talks and interviews given by Mother Teresa, and from letters, including *Co-Worker* newsletters, written by her.